Every Dog's Dream Rescue

A portion of all profits earned from your purchase of this book will be sent to Every Dog's Dream Rescue, Inc., a group of compassionate volunteers working around the clock to provide a safe haven for all the animals that are bought into their rescue facility. Every Dog's Dream not only maintains high-quality care for rescued dogs; they also take in cats and small animals. They operate an adoption center located within the Petco facility on Harry L. Drive in Johnson City, New York, where they always have an abundance of cats and kittens and a number of puppies up for adoption. Every Dog's Dream helps families across New York State to care for stray cats. They also help provide food and veterinary care for those who cannot afford to pay but don't want to give up their animals.

To find out more or to donate, go to: EveryDogsDream.org

Caring for Farm Animals

Village Earth Press

Copyright © 2017 by Village Earth Press, a division of Harding House Publishing.

All rights reserved. No part of this publication may be reproduced or transmitted in any form or by any means, electronic or mechanical, including photocopying, recording, taping, or any information storage and retrieval system, without permission from the publisher.

Village Earth Press
Vestal, New York 13850
www.villageearthpress.com

First Printing
9 8 7 6 5 4 3 2 1

ISBN: 978-1-62524-453-6
series ISBN: 978-1-62524-449-9

Author: Rae Simons
Design: Micaela Grace Sanna

Caring for Farm Animals

RAE SIMONS

TABLE OF CONTENTS:

Introduction	10
1. The Animals That Changed the World	14
2. Raising Poultry	28
3. Raising Livestock	42
4. Caring for Horses, Ponies, and Donkeys	52

Introduction

To parents and teachers:

• •

Animal lives matter. Human welfare and animal welfare are interwoven so tightly that they cannot be separated. In other words, what hurts animals will ultimately hurt us as well.

We can see this at the planetary level. As animals lose their habitats because of climate change, pollution, deforestation, and other factors, human well-being is also threatened. Sometimes, people seem to think it's an either-or situation: we either help people (by investing in businesses that are harming the environment) or we help animals (by hindering the success of those same businesses). That's not the way things work on our planet, though. We are all in this together. What puts animals at risk is an equal risk to human well-being.

We are not only linked to animals at the biological and environmental level. We also share many of the same emotions with them—and how we treat animals can't be separated from how we treat each other. Mark Bekoff, an evolutionary biologist, said in an interview with *Forbes* magazine:

> how we treat other animals has direct effects on how we feel about ourselves ...compassion begets compassion.... So, when we're nice to other animals and empathize compassionately with their physical and mental health we're also spreading compassion to other people.

The more scientists learn about animals, the more they find that the creatures with whom we share our planet are far more amazing than we ever knew. Scientists have proven that even fish are conscious and sentient; they've discovered that it's not only our dogs who are sensitive to our pain but that rats, mice, and even chickens are as well; and they also have proof that crows can use tools that are more sophisticated than chimpanzees'. What's more, based on animals' neurochemicals, our furred and feathered friends experience the same feelings of love that humans do.

Earlier cultures thought of animals as our brothers and sisters, but somehow, our culture lost track of that perspective. We need to regain it, not only for animals' sakes but for our own—and we need to teach it to our children. By teaching children how to care for animals (whether pets, farm animals, or wild animals), we are empowering children to become kinder and more responsible.

Psychologists, educators, and other experts agree. The National PTA Congress wrote:

> Children trained to extend justice, kindness, and mercy to animals become more just, kind, and considerate in their relations to each other. Character training along these lines will result in men and women of broader sympathies; more humane, more law abiding, in every respect more valuable citizens.

When children learn compassion and respect for animals, they are better able to extend compassion and respect to each other. A relationship with an animal also helps children gain self-confidence; research even indicates that being with an animal helps children relax and learn better. And by speaking out for those who cannot speak for themselves, children learn leadership and the power of their own voices to make the world a better place.

Village Earth Press has created this series of books because we believe that we need to take action on animals' behalf. We also believe that children should have opportunities to become all they can be. Our hope is that this book will contribute to both those goals.

Read more on this topic (and then discuss with children what you learn). We recommend these books:

The Emotional Lives of Animals
by Mark Bekoff

The Ten Trusts: What We Must Do to Care for the Animals We Love
by Jane Goodall

The Pig Who Sang to the Moon: The Emotional World of Farm Animals
by Jeffrey Moussaieff Masson

The Bond: Our Kinship with Animals, Our Call to Defend Them
by Wayne Pacelle

chapter 1
The Animals Who Changed the World

When your family needs food, you probably go to the grocery store. When you need clothes, you go to another store, and when you need medicine, you go to a still another store. Or you might go to one really big store that has food, clothes, medicine, and all sorts of other things. Stores are where most people today get the things they need.

But if you had been alive 15,000 years ago, your life would have been very different. There were no stores then. People got the things they needed—food, clothing, medicine, and pretty much everything else—from wild animals and plants.

Imagine you were alive back then. Your family would be part of a larger group of people who went wherever they could find food. This meant you didn't live in one place in a house. Instead, your people set up shelters wherever they stopped. The men hunted wild bison, sheep, and goats. The women gathered plants for food and medicine. The women also made food and clothing from the animals the men killed. When the herds of animals moved to a different place, your people packed up and moved too. You never stayed in one place very long.

You and your people paid close attention to Nature. You knew that without Nature, you would die. You **honored** the animals and plants that helped keep you alive. But the only tame animals you had were dogs. Dogs helped the men hunt. All other animals in the world were wild.

If you had gone forward in time and seen a farm, you wouldn't have understood what it was. And if you'd gone even further forward in time and seen a big store like a Walmart—or even a tiny little shop—filled with all kinds of food and other goods, you wouldn't have been able to believe your eyes. No one had ever dreamed of such a thing!

People who depend on Nature for their food are called hunters and gatherers. They don't have farms. Instead, they hunt and gather whatever

What's that mean?

When you HONOR someone or something, you think well of them. You pay attention to them. You treat them with respect.

What's that mean?

DOMESTICATE means to make an animal tame, so that it lives with humans.

MANURE is the poop that farm animals make.

To **FERTILIZE** means to add something to soil so that the plants that are planted there will grow better.

SLEDGES are like big sleds that are pulled by an animal.

Nature has to offer. Today only a very few people on Earth live like this. But many thousands of years ago, all humans were hunters and gatherers.

Then about 11,000 years ago, things began to change. Humans realized that if they planted the food they needed, they wouldn't have to be always searching for wild plants to eat. And if they could **domesticate** animals, people wouldn't have to pack up and move every time the herds moved. They could settle down and live in one place.

The first animals that were domesticated as a source of food were sheep in the Middle East. Goats were the next animals to be tamed. Now people kept large flocks of sheep and goats. People still moved around, though, because they went wherever there was fresh grass for their flocks.

Before long, people realized that these animals were not only good for food. Sheep and goats also made milk—and people could make the milk into cheese. Sheep's wool could be turned into yarn and woven into cloth.

Soon after this, cows and pig were also domesticated. Now, people started to settle down and live in one place. They planted crops. They used their animals' **manure** to **fertilize** their fields. Their animals also gave them leather—made from animal skins—to use for clothes and other things. Animal horns and bones could be used to make needles, weapons, and jewelry. Animal fat could be made into candles, so that people could have light at night.

As humans and animals lived together more and more, people realized that animals didn't have to be food in order to be useful. Animals like cows were big and strong. Now that cows were tame, they could be put to work. People made harnesses for them out of strips of leather. They used these strips of leather to fasten the cows—called oxen—to **sledges**. People could put loads of crops or wood or stone on the sledges, and the oxen would drag them. This meant people could get more work done faster. They could carry larger loads farther.

Life was changing a lot for human beings. Before long, they invented the wheel—and now oxen could pull wagons,

Did You Know?

Books were once written on animal skins instead of paper.

In India and Southeast Asia, people kept water buffalo instead of oxen. These animals gave milk, and they were also big and strong. They were good for hauling carts and pulling plows. Today, many farmers in these parts of the world still use water buffalo for plowing.

which worked even better than sledges. Oxen could also pull **plows**. Using plows meant people could plant more crops. They could spread their fields out further away from their homes, because now they could carry their crops home in wagons pulled by oxen. The world was changing because of people's new ideas—but none of it would have been possible without animals.

The next animal to be domesticated was the horse. Thousands of years ago, wild horses lived in most parts of the world, but more lived on the wide, flat lands of Asia than anywhere else. There

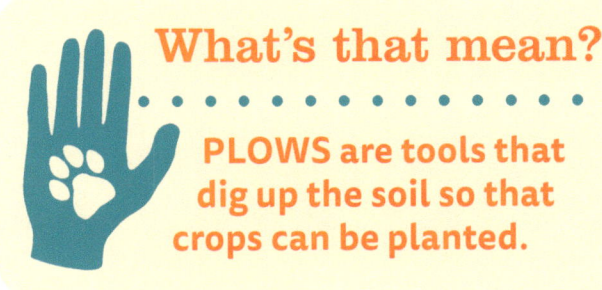

What's that mean?

PLOWS are tools that dig up the soil so that crops can be planted.

The Animals Who Changed the World • 17

Because camels can go a long time without water, camels could carry both people and loads over long distances. Camel caravans linked together parts of the world that had once been separated. Now, people in India could trade their goods with people in Egypt. Once again, animals changed the world!

Did You Know?

In some parts of the world, camels and their cousins the llamas were nearly as important as horses and donkeys.

the horses had plenty of room to gallop. They had lots of grass to eat. This is where humans first captured horses.

At first, people thought of horses as food, the same as cows or goats. Then people realized that horses could do something else for humans. People could ride horses. This meant that for the first time humans could travel greater distances far more quickly than ever before. When horses and people became friends, humans' lives changed forever.

At about the same time that wild horses were being tamed, their cousin the donkey was domesticated in Egypt, in the northern part of Africa. Donkeys weren't as fast as horses—but they were good at carrying heavy loads for long distances. Like horses, donkeys became humans' partners.

In India, people tamed elephants. Not only are elephants big and strong, able to carry people and loads, but they can also pick up heavy things with their trunks. Their trunks make them even better work partners for humans.

People in South America used llamas to carry heavy loads, the way people in other parts of the world used donkeys.

The first tame horses were the size of what we call ponies. These small wild horses are nearly extinct, but they still live in Asia on nature preserves.

The Animals Who Changed the World

> ### What's that mean?
>
> **DESCENDENTS** are children, grandchildren, great-grandchildren, great-great-grandchildren, and so on.
>
> **POULTRY** is a word for domesticated birds that are raised for food and eggs—for example, chicken, ducks, geese, and turkeys.

Humans and donkeys lived and worked together.

The last farm animals humans tamed were birds. The first domesticated bird was probably the red jungle fowl. People captured these birds and then kept them for both their meat and their eggs. All chickens in the world today are **descendents** of these birds.

Chickens aren't the only domesticated **poultry**. At about the time red jungle fowl were being tamed in Asia, people in Egypt were persuading pigeons to live with them for the same reasons—for meat and eggs. A thousand or so years later, on the other side of the world, the Aztecs in Mexico tamed wild turkeys.

Red jungle fowl still live in the forests and jungles of India and Southeast Asia.

The Spanish explorers who came to the Americas in the sixteenth century brought turkeys back with them to Europe. Then, when English settlers came to what is now the United States, they brought these tame turkeys with them on their ships. The tame turkeys had babies with the wild turkeys that already lived in the settlers' new home. Three hundred years later, we eat those turkeys' descendants for Thanksgiving dinner!

The Aztecs didn't eat their turkeys. Instead, they raised turkeys for their feathers. The Aztecs made headdresses and clothing from turkey feathers.

Timeline

20,000 years ago
Humans hunt large mammals.

12,000–16,000 years ago
Dogs are domesticated and help humans hunt.

9,000–12,000 years ago
Sheep, goats, cows, and pigs are domesticated.

About 6,000 years ago
Humans begin using oxen to pull sledges.

About 5,500 years ago
The wheel is invented, and people use oxen to pull wagons.

About 5,000 years ago
People begin to ride horses and donkeys.

More than 4,000 years ago
The plow is invented, and people begin using oxen, horses, and donkeys to pull plows.

About 3,500 years ago
People begin riding camels.

About 4,500 years ago
People capture wild elephants, tame them, and use them to carry people and loads.

About 4,000 years ago
Humans domesticate poultry.

About 3,000 years ago
The Aztecs in South Africa domesticate turkeys for their feathers.

The Animals Who Changed the World

Elephants

There are two kinds of elephants, the African elephant and the Indian elephant. Until recently, the Indian elephant was the only one that had been tamed, but African elephants can also be tamed and trained. For hundreds of years, people have used Indian elephants in wars, on farms, and as transportation. Unlike other farm animals that are bred by people, elephants are usually born in the wild and then captured and trained. African elephants and Indian elephants both perform in circuses. Because they are so smart, they learn tricks easily—but many elephants in circuses are treated cruelly.

Today, we may buy our food in stores—but our food still comes from plants and animals. Farms raise animals and grow crops that become the food we eat. But in many parts of the world, farming has changed a lot from the way it used to be.

Even fifty years ago, most farms all over the world were fairly small. They belonged to families who took care of their animals. Animals had room to move around. They lived outside in good weather, and in bad weather they had snug barns to shelter them. Most people were kind to their animals. People understood that animals were their partners in life. Even though the world had changed so much, people still knew they would not be alive without animals.

Today, though, many farm animals lives in places that are more like factories than farms. Instead of families, big companies own these enormous factory farms. The companies want to raise as many animals as they can, as quickly as they can, so they can make more money. Thousands of farm animals live squashed together in buildings. The animals don't go outside. They don't get to feel the sunshine. They can't run or play or do any of the things that all animals like to do. Their owners don't treat them like creatures who have feelings. Factories are places where things go in looking one way, and then they come out turned into something that people can sell and use. That's how many farm

Did You Know?

Pigs are very smart—as smart as dogs.

animals are treated today—as things that can be turned into something people will want to buy, things like hamburgers and hotdogs and chicken nuggets. Animals are not treated like living things.

Because of the cruel way that farm animals are often treated, some people believe it's wrong to eat meat. These people are called vegetarians. Other people don't eat eggs, milk, or any other food that comes from an animal, and these people are called vegans. Vegans eat only foods that come from plants.

How we treat animals is important. What we eat is important too. As you get older, you will need to decide for yourself what you feel is right when it comes to eating animals. But whatever you decide, it's never right to treat an animal cruelly. All animals have feelings. They feel pain. They get scared. They feel happy. Many scientists believe animals even feel love. Animals deserve to be treated with kindness and respect. We need to honor their lives.

So the next time you walk through a grocery store, take another look at the shelves. See that can of chicken noodle soup? Without a living, breathing, clucking chicken, that can wouldn't be there. How about that package of macaroni and cheese? Without a cow to give milk, there wouldn't be any cheese. Or that box of

waffles? Not only is it made from flour that comes from wheat plants, but it also contains eggs that come from chickens, as well as milk from cows. Sausages? They come from pigs. Ham? That comes from a pig too. Spaghettios with meatballs? Those meatballs came from a cow—one of those big gentle animals that moo and eat hay.

We need to remember that farm animals are our partners in life. They help feed us. We share our planet with them. For thousands of years, they have made human life possible. They helped us change our world.

And they can also make really good pets!

The Animals Who Changed the World

Chapter 2
Raising Poultry

Chicks and ducklings are very cute. They look like little balls of fluff with shiny bright eyes. But they're not toys! You should never get a baby chicken or duck unless you're sure you want to be responsible for an adult bird for its entire life. When people take good care of them, poultry can make good pets.

Ducks and chicken are two of the most common poultry, but there are other kinds too. Geese and turkeys are poultry. There are also less common kinds of poultry—like guinea fowl and partridges. Even giant ostriches are sometimes called poultry. Any birds that are raised for food (either as meat or for their eggs) are called poultry.

All poultry need a **coop** to live in, but they also need to be able to go outside. Ducks need water to splash in (even if it's just a kiddie pool). Chickens and other poultry love to scratch in the dirt for worms and bugs.

People who have chickens don't always live in the country. Some people keep chickens in their backyards. Even

big cities may allow you to keep a few chickens in your yard. Other towns and cities have rules against keeping poultry, so always check with your town or city offices before you bring home any kind of poultry.

One of the best things about poultry, of course, is that they will give you eggs. Not just chickens lay eggs. So do ducks, geese, and turkeys. Female poultry lay eggs even without a male bird around. Without a father bird, the eggs will never turn into baby birds. But they will be good to eat! One chicken will usually give you more than 200 eggs in a year. Duck eggs are good to eat too. In fact, any kind of bird egg can be eaten.

What's that mean?

A COOP is a special little house for poultry. Different kinds of poultry like different kinds of coops. If you want to raise poultry, do your research and find out what kind of house your birds will need.

Raising Poultry

Here are some things to keep in mind if you think you'd like to have poultry for pets:

- Baby poultry don't cost very much—but you will need to spend money on their food for the rest of their lives. Make sure the grown-ups in your family will help you get your pet poultry the food they need to be healthy.

- It's a good idea to get poultry when they are babies. Baby birds "bond" with the people who take care of them. This means they will learn to love you if you spend time and take care of them when they are little.

- If you are getting chickens, get girls. Boy chicks grow up to be roosters, and roosters aren't as friendly as hens. They're also noisy in the morning!

- Baby poultry need to be kept warm. They should live in a crate inside until they are old enough to go outside. At first, when they are very small, they will need a lamp over the crate to keep them warm. Keep them safe from any other pets you have.

- You will need to buy or build a coop. Make sure you get the right kind and size for your poultry.

- If your poultry is allowed to wander around the yard, they will find lots of things to eat on their own, but you will still need to feed them every day. You can find their food at a farm store.

- You need to make sure your birds always have fresh water to drink.

- You will need to keep their coop clean. You will also need to clean up their poop from the ground. Poultry can make a lot of poop!

- Make sure everyone in your family is ready to help take care of animals that might live as long as 10 years.

Did You Know?

A girl chicken is called a hen, and a boy chicken is a rooster. A female duck is also called a hen, but a male is called a drake. Baby geese are called goslings, and male geese are called ganders.

There are hundreds of chicken breeds, and some of them make better pets than others. These chickens are usually friendly, calm birds:

Plymouth Rock

Plymouth Rock hens are gentle birds that get along well with people and other animals. They lay four or five eggs a week.

Buff Orpington

These are large chickens that are friendly and loving. They even like to be held in people's arms! They lay about three eggs a week.

Brahma

These chickens come in two sizes—medium and small. Because their feathers grow over their feet, they look a little like they're wearing slippers. They don't mind being handled, and they can even be trained. Even Brahma roosters are usually friendly and gentle.

Silkie Bantam

These are tiny chickens with fluffy feathers that feel silky soft. They are easy to handle and make good pets—but they don't lay as many eggs as other kinds of chickens.

 **There are also different kinds of ducks. Some can fly and some can't. These ones cannot fly, and they make good pets:**

Pekins

These are large white ducks, and their ducklings are yellow. They are calm birds, and they like people, but they can be noisy.

Cayuga

These ducks have beautiful green feathers. They are the quietest kind of duck. If you have close neighbors who might be bothered by loud duck noises, Cayugas could be a good choice.

Campbell

These ducks are gentle and friendly. They don't mind living with chickens. They also lay as many eggs as a chicken does in a year. This duck is going for a swim in a kiddie pool.

Indian Runner

These funny-looking ducks don't swim, but they do like to stick their heads in a bucket of water. Because of their long necks, they need a taller coop than other poultry do. They're very tame—and funny to watch! They like to have a friend, so you should get two or three.

Other kinds of poultry can be kept as pets too:

Geese

Geese are larger than either chickens or ducks. If a goose grows up with you from the time she is a baby, she will love you and follow you around. Geese are intelligent, and they also make good "guard dogs." They can be very noisy, though, and they may attack people they don't know. They can live 15 to 20 years.

Turkeys

Turkeys can make good pets. They're big birds, so they need plenty of room to wander around and a house that's big enough for them. They eat almost anything, including table scraps. It's not a good idea to get a turkey if you're going to have chickens too, because turkeys who live with chickens can get sick and die.

Guinea Fowl

Guinea fowl are another kind of poultry that people sometimes keep as pets. They are funny, noisy birds that will eat all the bugs in your yard. Some people love guinea fowl, but others think they are too loud. These birds need lots of space, and they can fly away if their wings aren't clipped. If they are raised from the time they are babies with people and other animals or poultry, they usually get along well with everyone.

Peacocks

Peacocks are beautiful birds that can live in both hot and cold weather. They need many of the same things as other poultry, but they do need more space than other kinds of poultry. Peacocks aren't good pets if you have neighbors, because they have a very loud cry that sounds like someone screaming. They need at least an acre of fenced land with trees. Peacocks like to be up high at night, so they perch on tree branches when they sleep.

Raising Poultry

Did You Know?

Chickens are related to dinosaurs.

36 • CARING FOR FARM ANIMALS

Poultry are usually friendly birds. They like people, and they will often follow their owners around. When they see you, they may come running. They will "talk" to you (clucking, quacking, honking, or gobbling).

Like all pets, poultry need people to take care of them. They need somewhere to live that's protected from **predators**, like foxes and hawks. They need to be fed and given fresh water. They need to have clean houses where they can find shelter from the cold or the rain.

Poultry can make good pets—but they're not like cats or dogs. They're like themselves! If you are always kind and gentle to them, they will learn to trust you. They will like to be with you.

Poultry are lovable, chatty animals. If you and your family decide to get one or two (or a few) as pets, they will give you eggs and be your friends. And they'll count on you to take care of them. They'll need YOU.

What's that mean?

PREDATORS are animals that catch and eat other animals.

Here are books and websites that will help you and your family learn more about keeping poultry as pets:

A Kid's Guide to Keeping Chickens: Best Breeds, Creating a Home, Care and Handling, Outdoor Fun, Crafts and Treats
by Melissa Caughey

Pip! Zip! Hatch! Love!: A Complete Kid's Guide to Keeping Chickens
by Susanne Blummer

How to Raise a Chicken as a Family Pet
www.backyardchickens.com/a/how-to-raise-a-chicken-as-a-family-pet

Quack! A Quick Guide to Raising Ducks
www.organicauthority.com/pets/quick-guide-raising-ducks.html

My Pet Chicken
www.mypetchicken.com

Chapter 3
Raising Livestock

People use the word "livestock" to talk about all farm animals. The word "stock" means something that's valuable. When you put it together with the word "live," it's like saying farming animals are living, breathing money. Back in the days when most people were farmers, someone who had a lot of farm animals was usually rich. People needed animals for food. They would pay farmers for the milk and meat from their animals. This would make the farmers rich.

Today, there are still big farms that make money by raising animals. The farmers kill the animals and sell them for meat. Cows are raised for milk, but they are also raised to eat. When you eat beef, you are eating a cow. When you eat pork or bacon or ham, you are eating a pig. Goats are sometimes raised for their milk and sometimes for their meat. Sheep are raised both for their wool and for their meat.

You may not have been around farm animals very often. Unless you live on a farm, you may have only seen these animals in pictures or at a petting zoo. You may see them in a field when you go past in a car. When you think of getting a pet, you probably don't think about getting a cow or a pig!

If you live in an apartment building, then a farm animal is definitely not the right pet for you. But farm animals can be as smart and loving as cats and dogs. That doesn't mean a farm animal is the right pet for most people, though. Farm animals need outdoor space. They need care. Having a farm animal for a pet is a big, big responsibility.

Farm animals need a place to **graze** that is fenced, so they won't wander way. Like all animals, they need food and water every day. They need a shelter—a barn or a big shed—where they can get out of the cold, rain, and snow. They need to have their shelter cleaned, because farm animals make a LOT of poop! The bigger the animal, the more poop they'll make. That's one reason you probably shouldn't get a cow for a pet!

But if you live in the sort of place where you can give farm animals all the things they need—and if the grown-ups in your family want to help you!—these animals could become good friends that will love you their whole lives.

Pigs

Do you think of pigs as fat, dirty animals? That's not really true. Pigs

What's that mean?

When animals GRAZE, they eat grass and other plants growing from the ground.

Raising Livestock

actually don't like being dirty. If they have the chance, they are very clean animals. They are also very smart. In fact, pigs are smarter than many dogs are. Cats and dogs don't understand mirrors, but pigs do. Pigs know that when they look in a mirror, they are seeing themselves! They can also be taught tricks, and they like to play games. They like to play with balls and toys, just like dogs do. (They don't usually like to play "fetch," though.) Pigs get bored and sad if they don't have something interesting to do. They can also be **housetrained**, just like dogs and cats can. Pigs can even be trained to walk on a leash.

More and more people are deciding that pigs make good pets. Pot-bellied pigs are a kind of pig that has become quite common as a pet. Pigs don't shed fur like dogs do. They don't bark, they don't smell bad the way a dog can, and they don't get fleas. Their poop is easier to clean up than a dog's. Those are all good things!

But pigs aren't dogs. They're not happy living inside most of the time, the way a dog is. Pigs need to be outside and have space to **root**. They'll need an outdoor house (a shed or a doghouse) where they can go to get out of the sun and the cold. Some pet pigs live outside during the day and then come in at night to sleep with their people. Other pigs really want to live outside all the time. You shouldn't get a pet pig unless you have plenty of outdoor space. Pigs will also be happier—and less likely to get in trouble—if they have a friend. It's a good idea to get two pigs at once.

Pigs need to eat grain, vegetables, and some fruit. You can buy special pig feed at most pet stores or at farm stores, but you should also give your

What's that mean?

HOUSETRAINED means that an animal has been taught to only poop and pee in a special box or outdoors.

When a pig ROOTS, she pushes her nose into the dirt. Pigs need to root because they get things from soil they need to be healthy. It's what they do instead of taking a vitamin pill!

40 • CARING FOR FARM ANIMALS

Sheep and goats are called "herd" animals. That means they're used to living in groups of other goats and sheep. You should always get two or three sheep or goats, because one by himself would be sad and lonely.

pet pig "people" vegetables, like fresh carrots, spinach, cucumbers, and celery. Pigs will also eat table scraps—but it's not a good idea.

Canned vegetables, corn and potatoes, cookies, and junk food could make your pig fat. Don't use your pig as a garbage disposal! And always make sure he has plenty of fresh water.

Sheep and Goats

Sheep and goats aren't indoor animals. They can't be housetrained. They don't need a lot of outdoor room, though. They can be quite happy living in a backyard. They'll need a shelter, of course, but a small shed will be enough. They don't need a big barn like cows would.

Raising Livestock

Because goats are so good at solving puzzles, they're also escape artists. They're good at finding ways to get out of their pen or barn. You have to be careful, because they can learn to lift latches with their noses!

Sheep and goats can't be trained the way you would a dog—but they're still smart. Sheep recognize faces. Goats can solve puzzles. They love their owners. They can make friends with other animals.

Sheep and goats eat hay. They also eat special feed you can buy at a farm store. They need fresh, clean water every day.

Goats and sheep can live together happily. They need many of the same things. They also need some different things.

Goats love to climb, so they like a pile of rocks to play on. They'll be just as happy with a picnic table or anything else they can jump on and off. Male goats smell really bad—so if you have a boy goat, you should have him neutered.

Sheep need to be sheared. This means they need to have their wool cut off once a year. During the winter, their wool gets thick to keep them warm. When summer comes, they'll be hot and miserable if it's not cut off. Imagine how you would feel wearing a wool sweater all summer long! Shearing a sheep isn't something you should try to do yourself. You would need to find someone in your area who knows how to do it. The wool can then be washed and spun into yarn.

If you and your family decide to get a farm animal as a pet, you'll need to be ready to take care of that animal for the rest of its life. Most farm animals live more than ten years, so it's a big

responsibility. You can't go away and leave them without someone to take care of them. You'll have to have a veterinarian come to see them if they get sick. They need shots, just like dogs and cats (and you) do. They may also need their hooves trimmed by a veterinarian. This is kind of like clipping your fingernails or toenails! Some farm animals' hooves keep growing all the time the same way your nails do. Veterinarians cost money, so make sure the grown-ups in your family will help you pay for your animals' care.

Here are questions you and your family should answer before deciding to get a farm animal:

- Does your town or city allow farm animals? You'll need to call your town or city offices to make sure they don't have a law against people having farm animals.

- Have you spent time with the animal you're thinking of getting as a pet? It's a good idea to visit someone who already has this kind of animal as a pet. That way you will understand better what this animal is like. You may think the animal is very cute—but it might turn out that it's not the right pet for you.

- Are you ready to have two animals? Most farm animals need a friend. Otherwise, they're lonely and sad.

- Would you be better off getting a dog or cat? Dogs or cats are lots of work too, of course, but they usually fit into people's lives a little more easily than farm animals do.

- Do you have enough patience and time to give your farm animals?

- Do you have enough outdoor space for your farm animals?

- Does your family plan to move in the next ten years? If so, will you be able to move somewhere your farm animals will still have outdoor space?

- Do you have enough money for your farm animals' veterinary care?

- Do you have someone who can take care of your farm animals if you go away?

- Have you thought through this decision carefully? Have you found out everything you can about what these animals need? Do you understand the responsibility you're taking on?

Livestock—or Pets?

Once you have a farm animal for a pet, you may not ever want to eat that kind of animal again. It's hard to eat something once you know that it's

smart and has feelings, just like dogs and cats—and just like people.

Some people still feel it's okay to eat animals. That's a decision you'll have to make for yourself. But whether you eat animals or not, ALL animals need to be treated with kindness and respect. Many animals that are eaten as meat have unhappy lives. They are treated cruelly.

Even if you think farm animals are food, they AREN'T living money. They deserve good care just as much as cats and dogs and all other animals do. If

Cows are too big to make good pets for most people. Taking care of a cow is a lot of work. But cows are sweet, loving animals. They have good memories, and they make friends with each other and with people. They can remember faces.

Raising Livestock

Did You Know?

Pigs don't sweat—but they do get sunburned. They don't roll in mud because they are dirty. They do it to keep cool. The mud keeps the sun from burning their skin. It's like suntan lotion for pigs!

There are shelters and sanctuaries that take in farm animals. If you decide you want farm animals as pets, get them from one of these places. That way you will be giving a good home to animals that really need it.

you decide to eat meat, make sure that the animals were treated well before they died. This means you'll have to ask lots of questions. Do your *research*. Find out where your meat came from. Meat doesn't start out in a plastic package at the grocery store. It starts out as a living, breathing animal.

You may decide a farm animal isn't the right pet for you. But farm animals still need you. They need you to learn about their lives—and then they need you to speak out for them. The more you tell your friends and family about farm animals, the more they will know too. And the more people know and care about farm animals, the more we can all work together to make sure these animals have good lives.

> ## What's that mean?
>
> When you RESEARCH something, you find out all about it. You ask questions about it—and then you find the answers. You read about it online. You go to the library or the bookstore and find books about it. You ask people who know about it to tell you everything they know.

YOU have the power to make a difference.

Here are books and websites that will help you and your family learn more about farm animals:

The Backyard Goat: An Introductory Guide to Keeping & Enjoying Pet Goats
by Sue Weaver

Barnyard Kids: A Family Guide for Raising Animals
by Dina Rudick

Compassionate Farming Education Initiative
www.compassionatefarming.org

Farm Sanctuary
www.farmsanctuary.org

Pig Placement Network
www.pigplacementnetwork.com

Raising Livestock   47

Caring for Horses, Ponies, and Donkeys

chapter 4

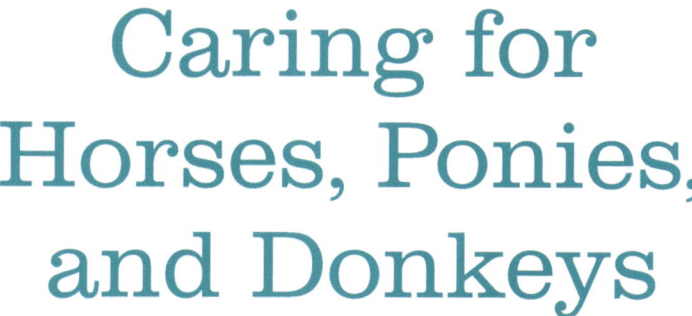

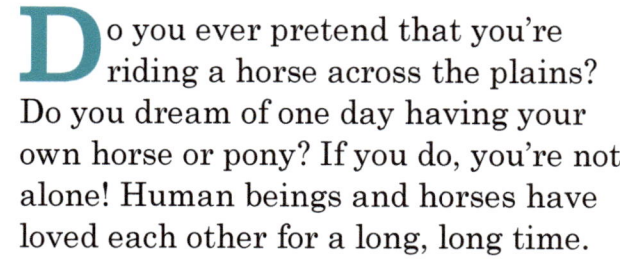

Do you ever pretend that you're riding a horse across the plains? Do you dream of one day having your own horse or pony? If you do, you're not alone! Human beings and horses have loved each other for a long, long time.

Up until about a hundred years ago, most households had at least one horse. Having a horse then was like having a car today. People needed horses to get them where they wanted to go. If they lived in the county and they wanted to go to town, they had to hitch up their horse to their wagon. If they had more money and they lived in a city, they probably had a horse to pull their **buggy**. People also rode their horses. Some people—like farmers and cowboys—used their horses to help them do their work.

Today, we don't need horses to pull our wagons and carriages. People still like to ride horses, though, because it's fun. And people still love horses. Most of today's horses are really pets. They don't have a job they have to do.

If you think you might like to have a horse or pony of your own, there are

lots of things you'll need to think about first. For one thing, horses and ponies usually cost a lot more than many other kinds of pets. You won't be able to save up your allowance to buy one. A well-bred horse can cost anywhere between $1000 and $8000! Ponies are cheaper. Although some ponies are very expensive, you can also buy ponies that cost between $300 and $1000.

Buying your horse or pony is just the first cost you'll have to pay. Horses and ponies also cost a lot to take care of. There are a lot of things you'll have to do. They are big animals, so they eat a lot food. They need a lot of space.

What's that mean?

A BUGGY was a kind of small carriage that was usually pulled by just one horse.

Here are things your horse or pony will need:

- First of all, they need a field where they can move around. You'll need about one acre of fenced-in land.
- They need a shelter (usually called a "stable"). If you don't have room for a horse where you live, you might keep your horse somewhere else. This is called "boarding" your horse.

Caring for Horses, Ponies, and Donkeys

> **What's that mean?**
>
> **GROOMING** is how you keep a horse's coat shiny and clean.
>
> **TACK** is the equipment you need for riding a horse. The saddle, bridle, halter, stirrups, and saddle pad are all part of the tack.

There are special places that board horses. They may also help you take care of your horse by feeding and **grooming** her. All this can cost between $50 and $200 a month.

- Horses and ponies eat hay—a lot of hay! Depending on how big your horse is and how much she eats, her hay will cost between $100 and $200 a month.
- Horse and ponies also eat grain, which costs about $20 for a 50-pound bag. That might sound like a lot of grain—but it could only last your horse about three days! You'll need to spend another $100 or more a month on grain.
- If you want to ride your horse or pony, you'll need **tack**. If you plan to buy these new, they could cost between $400 and $1500. You could also find them used on Craigslist or at a pawnshop for a lot less than that.
- Your horse will need to be groomed with combs and brushes, which can cost about $50.
- Your horse will need to see a doctor—a veterinarian—just like you do. Vets that take care of horses come to wherever the horse lives. Your horse will need to have shots and a checkup once a year. If she gets sick, she'll also need the vet to come and help her get better. And on top of that, horses need to see a special dentist! All that can cost about $350 or more a year.
- Your horse's feet will also need care. If your horse has shoes nailed to her hooves, she'll need a farrier (someone who puts horseshoes on horses) to visit once every six weeks or so. She also needs her hooves trimmed. (It's a little like getting your fingernails clipped.) All of this will cost another $50 or so every month.

Did You Know?

The oldest horse lived to be 52 years old.

Horses, ponies, and donkeys are all friendly animals. When they were wild animals, they lived in herds. This means they don't like to live all alone. If you don't keep another animal with your horse or pony, she'll be sad and lonely. It doesn't have to be another horse, though. Lots of people have a goat to keep their horse company.

Caring for Horses, Ponies, and Donkeys

As you can see, having a horse or pony costs a lot of money! You'll need to be sure the grown-ups in your family are willing to pay all that money. If they can't afford it, don't be too disappointed! Having a horse is a big, expensive **responsibility**.

If you do decide to get a horse or pony, don't pick the one you think is prettiest. He may not be the right one for you. Here are some questions you should ask the person who is selling a horse or pony:

- Why are you selling your horse?
- How old is the horse?
- Is the horse used to being ridden?
- Would this be a good horse for a beginning rider?
- Does the horse like children?

What's that mean?

A RESPONSIBILITY is something you have to do, no matter what. Even on the days when you don't feel like doing it, you still have to.

The only real difference between horses and ponies is their size. Any horse that is shorter than 58 inches at the highest point of his back is considered a pony.

CARING FOR FARM ANIMALS

You don't have to ride a horse or pony to enjoy being with him. Some people keep horses and ponies that they don't ride. They just love them and like being with them.

- Does the horse get along with other animals?
- Does the horse go easily into a trailer? (This is important for moving your horse from place to place.)
- Does the horse have any bad habits?
- Does the horse get sick very often? Is there anything wrong with the horse?

Be careful not to buy an untrained horse or pony, even though they usually don't cost as much as other horses or ponies. These animals have never had anyone ride them. If you climbed on their back, they wouldn't understand what you wanted to do. They would probably try to get you off their back! It takes a long time to train a horse and it costs a lot of money.

You might want to consider getting an older horse. Horses and ponies live a long time, so if you were to get a horse that was 15 or 20 years old, she might live another 5, 10, or even 20 years. Ponies usually live a little longer than horses, so a pony that's more than 30 years old is usually still lively and friendly. Older horses don't cost as much, and they're usually calmer and more gentle than younger horses.

Your horse needs you to take care of her. Here are things you need to do:

- Feed your horse two to three times a day.
- Check your horse's water supply every day. Remember, all animals need water!
- Check to see if your horse looks sick. Is he limping? Does he act as though something hurts him? Is he coughing? Does his poop look the way it usually does — or is it runny and funny colored? All these things are signs that you need to call the vet to look at him.
- Exercise your horse at least 30 minutes every day.
- Give your horse a long workout that lasts a couple of hours at least once

What About Donkeys?

Donkeys also make wonderful pets. They don't cost as much as a horse or pony. They're easier to take care of. They don't mind the cold, and they don't need as much space as a horse or pony does. Some people ride larger donkeys, but many donkeys are just kept as pets. Because they are smaller than horses, they are easier to handle.

Donkeys are very smart. They are easy to train, like a dog, and they like to play. They even like to play with toys! They love people.

A donkey needs some of the same things a horse or pony does. He'll need to have his hooves trimmed, and he needs to have shots and see a vet once a year.

Donkeys are sometimes called burros. They come in different sizes. Larger ones can be as big as a large pony. Very small ones are called miniature donkeys. People always say that donkeys are stubborn. Really, though, donkeys are so smart that they like to make up their own minds about things. They won't do anything they think might be dangerous. While they're deciding what they want to do, you can't rush them!

Caring for Horses, Ponies, and Donkeys

a week. Horses need exercise (just like you do).

- Always walk your horse for a while after exercise, until he cools down and his breathing is relaxed and normal.

- Clean out your horse's stall every day. It's a dirty, smelly job—but if you don't do it, your horse could get sick.

- Groom your horse and clean her hooves at least once a week.

Llamas and Alpacas

A long time ago, people used horses, ponies, and donkeys to carry loads. In some parts of the world they still do—but in the mountains of South American llamas and alpacas do this job. (Alpacas are just like llamas only smaller.) Today, these animals have become popular pets. They're gentle and loving, and they get along well with other animals. Like horses and ponies, they need a field where they can move around—but they're easier to take care of and they don't eat as much as horses. They are also herd animals, so they don't like to live alone. They get along well with goats, horses, donkeys, and other animals. There are rescue organizations for llamas, just like there are for horse, ponies, and donkeys. If you adopt a llama or alpaca from one of these rescue organizations, you'll know you are giving a home to an animal that really needs one.

Did You Know? Donkeys and horses can be good friends.

When a donkey and a horse have a baby, it's called a mule. Mules are larger than donkeys. In this picture, a mule is on the left, a donkey on the right, and a horse in the background. In some parts of the world, people don't keep donkeys and mules as pets. Instead, they are work animals. Donkeys are very strong. They can carry heavy loads on their backs.

Good Friends

Horses were once considered farm animals. They helped farmers do their work by pulling plows and other farm equipment. Horses also went to war with people back in the days when wars were fought only on the ground. Warhorses were trained to handle the noise and sudden movements of war. Horses worked hard for humans—and humans and horses were often close friends.

Today, horses and humans are still good friends. Scientists have found that horses always remember the people they love, even when they haven't seen the people for a long time. Scientists have also found that being around horses is good for people. Spending time with a horse makes people feel happier and calmer. Being with a horse can even make people healthier.

Do you think you might like to have a horse friend? It's a big responsibility—

Caring for Horses, Ponies, and Donkeys

but having a horse friend can be wonderful.

You can get horses, ponies, or donkeys from rescue organizations that try to find homes for animals with no homes. These animals are much cheaper than other horses, ponies, and donkeys—and they need a good home! They just might need YOU!

An older horse can be a good friend, and you could have many good years with him. You will need to make sure a dentist looks at his mouth, because older horses can have sore teeth. If he does have sore teeth, you can feed him softer hay and put water in his grain. If it's cold out, make sure he has a shelter where he can get out of the cold. In the winter, you can give him a blanket to wear (like the one the horse is wearing here).

Did You Know?

There are about 200,000 horses and ponies in the United States that don't have homes. These animals need someone who will love them and take care of them.

Horses, ponies, and donkeys need to see a dentist regularly, just like you do. They can get toothaches and have other problems with their teeth. A horse dentist will make sure their teeth stay healthy.

Here are books and a website that will help you and your family learn more about having a pet horse, pony, donkey, or llama:

How to Speak "Horse": A Horse-Crazy Kid's Guide
by Andrea Eschbach

Llama Keeping: Raising Llamas—Step by Step Guide Book
by Harry Fields

Donkey Health and Welfare
www.thedonkeysanctuary.org.uk/donkey-health-and-welfare

Image Credits

Cover: Martine De Graaf (Dreamstime), Micaela Grace Sanna

Pages 1-4: Andreas Karelias (Dreamstime), AngelaLouwe (Shutterstock), Braendan Yong (Dreamstime), Chris Turner (Dreamstime), Eric Limon (Dreamstime), Imantsu (Dreamstime), Jason Bennée (Dreamstime), Joseph Golby (Dreamstime), Kalin Nedkov (Dreamstime), Maximilian Pogonii (Dreamstime), Micaela Grace Sanna, Mihocphoto (Dreamstime), Teresa Kenney (Dreamstime), Tilo (Dreamstime), Toa555 (Dreamstime), thanasit thinwongphet (Shutterstock)

Introduction: Micaela Grace Sanna, Viktoria Makarova (Dreamstime)

Chapter 1: Beat Germann (Dreamstime), Digitalpress (Dreamstime), Dutchscenery (Dreamstime), Eric Isselee (Shutterstock), Freder1 (Dreamstime), Isaxar (Dreamstime), Johncarnemolla (Dreamstime), Jose Tejo (Dreamstime), Khunaspix (Dreamstime), Mcherevan (Dreamstime), Micaela Grace Sanna, Noppadon Sangpeam (Dreamstime), Nostone (Dreamstime), Ronfromyork (Dreamstime), Zepherwind (Dreamstime)

Chapter 2: Duncan Noakes (Dreamstime), Elena Elisseeva (Dreamstime), Fotostraveller (Dreamstime), Irina Platner (Dreamstime), Iuliia Vasileva (Dreamstime), Kimi09 (Dreamstime), Luis Martinez (Dreamstime), Micaela Grace Sanna, Michael Haskin (Dreamstime), Mikelane45 (Dreamstime), Miroslav Hlavko (Dreamstime), Mollynz (Dreamstime), Scott Griessel (Dreamstime), Stefan Andronache (Dreamstime), Val Armstrong (Dreamstime)

Chapter 3: Clearviewstock (Dreamstime), Eric Isselee (Shutterstock), Fieldwork (Dreamstime), Heebyj (Dreamstime), Micaela Grace Sanna, Mysikrysa (Dreamstime), Photoinjection (Dreamstime), Sonsedska Yuliia (Shutterstock)

Chapter 4: Cynoclub (Dreamstime), Eric Isselee (Shutterstock), Fieldwork (Dreamstime), Heebyj (Dreamstime), Micaela Grace Sanna, Mysikrysa (Dreamstime), Robyn Mackenzie (Dreamstime), Sonsedska Yuliia (Shutterstock)

Chapter 5: Bruce Parrott (Dreamstime), Claudia Närdemann (Dreamstime), Erik Lam (Dreamstime), Jean Schweitzer (Dreamstime), Johann Helgason (Dreamstime), Micaela Grace Sanna, Olga Itina (Dreamstime), Thomas Males (Dreamstime)

Pages 61-64: Andrei Calangiu (Dreamstime), Carlos Restrepo (Dreamstime), Edurivero (Dreamstime), Elena Titarenco (Dreamstime), Elfrock (Dreamstime), Greenfire (Dreamstime), Grigor Atanasov (Dreamstime), Helena Bilková (Dreamstime), Ina Kozmina (Dreamstime), Martine De Graaf (Dreamstime), Micaela Grace Sanna, Mollynz (Dreamstime), Neil Denize (Dreamstime), Photomyeye (Dreamstime), Robert Hardholt (Dreamstime), Sebastian Czapnik (Dreamstime), Sebastianknight (Dreamstime), Toneimage (Dreamstime)

www.ingramcontent.com/pod-product-compliance
Lightning Source LLC
Chambersburg PA
CBHW061358090426
42743CB00002B/52